Dress-up Fashion

Things to make and do

Bath · New York · Singapore · Hong Kong · Cologne · Delhi
Melbourne · Amsterdam · Johannesburg · Auckland · Shenzhen

First published by Parragon in 2011

Parragon
Queen Street House
4 Queen Street
Bath BA1 1HE, UK

ISBN 978-1-4454-2161-2
Printed in China.

Contents

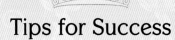

Getting started

Tips for Success

Remember, everything in this book should be made with the supervision and help of a grown up! A step labelled with "Kids" means that a child can do this step on their own. Some items will need to be purchased from a supermarket or a craft/hobby store.

1 Prepare your space

Cover your workspace with newspaper or a plastic or paper tablecloth. Make sure you are wearing clothes (including shoes!) that you don't mind becoming splattered with food, paint, or glue. But relax! You'll never completely avoid mess; in fact, it's part of the fun!

2 Wash your hands

Wash your hands before starting a new project, and clean up as you go along. Clean hands make for clean crafts! Remember to wash your hands afterwards too, using soap and warm water to remove any of the remaining materials.

3 Follow steps carefully

Follow each step carefully, and in the sequence in which it appears. We've tested all the projects; we know they work, and we want them to work for you, too.

♥ 4 Measure precisely

If a project gives you measurements, use your ruler, measuring scales, or measuring spoons to make sure you measure as accurately as you can. Sometimes, the success of the project may depend on it.

♥ 5 Be patient

You may need to wait while something bakes or leave paint, glue or clay to dry, sometimes for a few hours or even overnight. Be patient! Plan another activity while you wait, but it's important not to rush something as it may affect the outcome!

♥ 6 Clean up

When you've finished your project, clean up any mess. Store all the materials together so that they are ready for the next time you want to make and do. If you are making something with someone else then ensure it is a team effort!

Belle | *Rose Brooch*

Roses are very important to Belle. Breaking the spell on the enchanted rose meant that Belle could be with the Prince!

You will need

- A section cut from an egg carton
- Green paint
- Paintbrush
- Red felt 20 x 20 inches (50 x 50cm)
- Scissors
- Glue and tape
- A safety pin

1

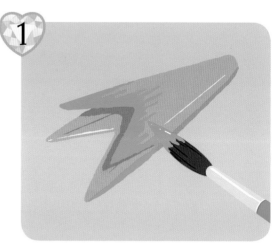

Cut off a single section from an egg carton. Cut the sides into points then paint it green to look like the bottom of a rose bud. Leave to dry.

2

Cut out ten circles from your red felt. These should have a diameter of 2¾ inches (7cm).

3

Roll up one of the felt circles. Stick some tape around one end. The felt should remain rolled up, but one end should be loose, forming the centre of your rose.

4

Glue the remaining felt circles around this middle piece to form your rose. These should start out quite tight until the outer circles are simply stuck on. Tape a safety pin to the egg carton, then glue the rose inside.

Belle's tip:
You can pin this rose to a top, a coat or even your bag. Beautiful!

Jasmine — Beautiful Fan

Jasmine loves living in such a hot place. But sometimes a Princess needs to cool down. This beautiful fan is perfect for hot weather or as a stylish accessory!

1

Draw three circles each 6 inches (15cm) in diameter on the cardboard. You could use a small plate as a guide. Cut out the circles. Paint in your favourite colours. Paint each side at a time allowing to dry.

You will need

- Thick cardboard
- Small plate
- Glue
- Pencil
- Paint
- 2 sticks
- Tape
- Ribbon
- Feathers
- Glitter glue

2

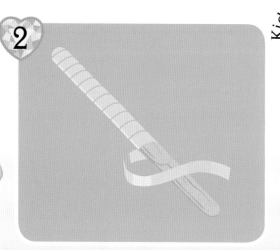

Tape two wooden sticks together, then wind some ribbon around the outside. Secure the ribbon ends in place with a dot of glue or tape.

3

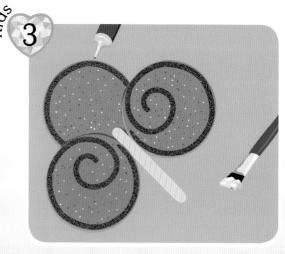

Glue the three circles together, arranging into a fan shape. Glue the stick into the middle. Using your glitter glue decorate the fan with a pretty pattern. Ensure this is left to dry.

4

Arrange feathers and gem on the fan. Glue feathers and gem to the fan when you are happy with the arrangement. Tie strips of ribbon to the bottom of the handle and stick another gem to the base where the ribbons join. Allow the glue to dry.

Tiana Celebration Mask

Tiana loves to wear a mask during Mardi Gras. You can make your own celebration mask for a special occasion or to put on your wall!

You will need

- Coloured card
- Pencil
- Feathers of mixed colours
- Sequins
- Scissors
- Glue
- Glitter glue
- Elastic

Fold a piece of 10 x 5 inches (25 x 12cm) card in half. Draw half a mask shape. Make the eye hole around 1 inch (3cm) from the folded edge. Cut out the mask outline and eye hole.

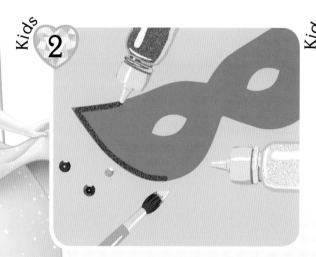

Decorate around the edge and eyes with glitter glue and allow to dry. Glue small sequins onto the mask to decorate. Leave to dry.

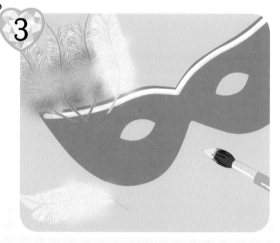

Turn the mask over and glue feathers along the top. Make sure they don't cover the eye holes. Allow to dry.

4

Make a small hole on each side of the mask. Thread a piece of elastic through each hole with a knot on the end. The knot should be tied on the reverse of the mask.

Tiana's tip:
You could make one of these for each of your friends, then take a picture of you all wearing them!

Aurora Flutter Butterfly Clips

Aurora loves to see the butterflies flutter around. Create these nature inspired butterfly hair clips and see them flutter and sparkle in your hair!

1

Fold a piece of 4¾ x 4 inches (12 x 10cm) paper in half. Draw half a butterfly shape along the fold, then cut it out.

You will need

- Card
- Coloured paper
- Pencil
- Glitter
- Glue
- Sequins
- Pipe cleaner
- A plain hair clip

2

Thinly brush glue over the butterfly. Don't use too much or it will curl up. Sprinkle different colours of glitter over the glue.

3

Bend a piece of pipe cleaner down the middle of the butterfly for the body. Twist the ends together around the back.

4

Aurora's tip:
Another idea you could
try is decorating a hair band.
Try one butterfly on the side
or stick a few across
the top!

Glue sequins for the eyes and spots,
add thin strips of coloured paper for the
antennae. Glue the finished butterfly onto
a plain hair clip. Leave to dry.

Castle Jewellery Stand

A castle is not just a castle, it is also a wonderful way to display your Princess fashion crafts and jewellery!

You will need

- A small cardboard box
- Cardboard tubes – different sizes
- A circular lid – for a balcony
- Coloured card (dark blue) for doors and windows
- Pencil
- Scissors
- Glue
- Masking tape
- Small saucers
- Paints
- Brushes
- Sequins/gems

1

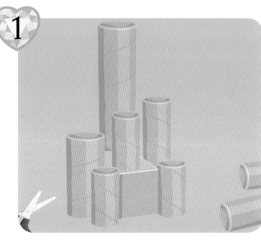

Arrange the tubes around a small box into a good castle shape. Cut the tubes if you need to so they vary in height. Don't glue them together yet.

2

Cut out some circles from card to make the turrets, they need to be around 14cm diameter for smaller turrets and 20 cm diameter for the bigger ones. Cut the circles in half so you have semi circles.

3

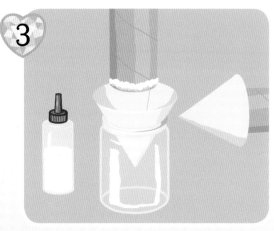

Curl the semi circles into cone shapes and stick masking tape along the edge. Place each cone upside down into a small jar (to stop it rolling around) then glue the tube inside it.

4

Glue the turrets together around the box. To make a balcony, glue a lid to the largest turret, then stick the small turret on top. Leave the glue to dry, then paint your castle in a beige colour to make it look like a castle wall.

5

When the paint has dried, glue the small windows and a door in place that you have cut out from the card. Glue sequins for extra sparkle. Then display your most precious jewellery from the turrets.

Snow White's tip: Put this castle somewhere prominent in your room. This castle really needs to be seen!

Tiana
Water Lily Apron

Tiana loves to cook! When you and someone special are baking wonderful treats together you'll both need an apron to protect your clothes.

1

Tape an ironed apron to a table with some card and newspaper underneath.

You will need

- A plain apron
- Masking tape
- A pencil
- Scissors
- Card
- Sponge
- Brushes
- Fabric paints

2

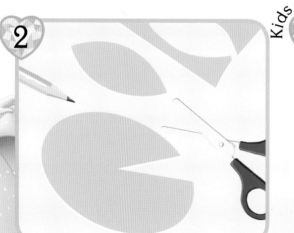

Draw a simple water lily petal shape onto card and also a lily pad shape. Cut them out.

Kids

3

Sponge some white paint onto the petal shaped card, then press it down in the centre of the apron. Repeat this until you have a flower, then leave to dry.

4

Sponge some pale green paint onto the card lily pad. Print it onto the apron, then flip it over to make another lily pad shape, then leave to dry.

5

Add a printed pattern to the centre of the flower with a strip of card with paint added to one edge, then paint yellow dots to finish the flower!

Tiana's tip:
As a special touch why not write their name on their new apron!

Sparkly Star Charm

Cinderella loves the sparkle of a night sky filled with stars. Make this star charm and add some sparkle to your wardrobe.

You will need

- Salt dough recipe:

  2 cups (200g) plain flour
  1 cup (200g) of salt
  1 cup (200ml) of water
  1 tablespoon of cooking oil

- A rolling pin
- Star shaped cookie cutters
- A cocktail stick
- Paint
- Brush
- Glue
- Gems
- A key chain or charm chain with a big jump ring

Kids

1

Mix up 2 cups (200g) of plain flour and 1 cup (200g) of salt in a mixing bowl. Add 1 cup (200ml) of water, and 1 tablespoon oil. Mix together into a smooth dough. If your dough is too sticky, add more flour, if it is too crumbly add more water.

2

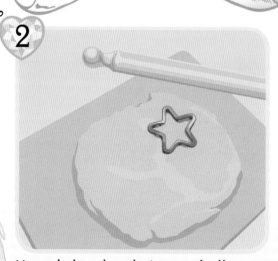

Knead the dough into a ball on a floured work surface. Roll it out to ½ inch (1cm) thick. Cut out shapes using small cookie cutters.

3

Make a hole in the top of each shape with a cocktail stick or pencil. Be sure it goes all the way through and doesn't close up. Leave to dry. It could take a few days normally or only a few hours in an oven on a very low temperature.

4

Paint the shapes and leave to dry then glue on gems and glitter. Fix a jump ring through the holes and then attach onto a key chain.

Cinderella's tip:
You could make a heart charm, just cut out heart shapes instead of stars!

19

Dazzling Tiaras

To dazzle like a princess you need a wonderful tiara to wear. Follow these steps and create a colourful piece of headware.

You will need

- Card
- Cup
- PVA glue
- Tissue paper
- Curly parcel string or ribbon
- Sweet wrappers
- Pipe cleaners or string
- Sticky tape
- Scissors

1

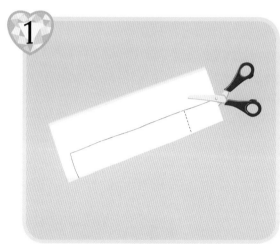

Cut a band of card 1 inch (3cm) wide and long enough to fit around your head with 1½ inches (4cm) overlap at the back. Leave flat. Paint the headband with glue and cover with a layer of tissue paper.

2

Leave it to dry. Then trim the edges with scissors to make it neat. Tape the parcel string or ribbon to the back of the headband at an angle. Wrap it around the headband and tape it at the other end.

3

Trace a small circle around a cup onto card. Cut it out. Paint it with glue. Cover it with tissue paper and leave it to dry. Trim the edges to make it neat.

Tape the circle face down on the centre back of the headband so that half the circle shows from the front. Now you are ready to decorate your tiara with gold hearts and a scrunched up sweet wrapper.

Ask someone to help you hold the band in place around your head and tape it together at the right size. Then take it off and tape the ends.

Jasmine's tip:
Here are some ideas for other tiaras you could try making.

Tiana *Pretty Necklace*

Now let's make pasta jewellery with Tiana. You can use these shapes and colours, or choose your own.

Kids

1

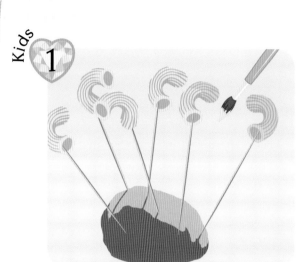

Paint the macaroni in a pink princess colour and leave to dry on top of toothpicks stuck into modelling clay. If you want, as an added option, you can add a coating of glue and glitter and leave to dry.

You will need

- Dried pasta shapes: 30 macaroni
- Acrylic paints: pastel pink Glitter and glue
- Lump of modelling clay
- Toothpicks
- Coloured string, elastic, or cord
- Button

2

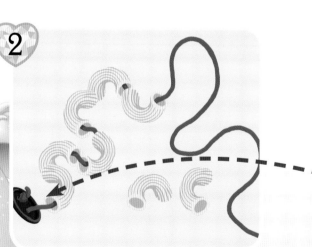

Tie a button to the string while you thread the shapes to keep them from falling off!

Thread each macaroni onto the coloured string or cord. Repeat this until all the pasta is threaded.

Tiana's tip:
There are a lot of
different pasta shapes, like
twirls or bow ties.
Try a different style like
in the picture!

Knot the two ends of the string together, making sure you have made your necklace big enough to go over your head.

Ocean Bracelet

Ariel is always so inspired by the ocean world. These beads are beautiful ocean blues, green and yellows!

1

Roll the three colours of clay into sausage shapes and put them side by side. Using a plastic knife, cut sections of about the same size through all three lengths together.

You will need

- Air–drying clay: green, yellow, turquoise
- Plastic knife
- 15 toothpicks
- Mug or glass
- Darning needle
- Thin elastic thread
- Scissors

2

Take a section and roll it into a ball between your palms until the colours are mixed together. Repeat until you have made about 15 balls.

Kids

3

Push a toothpick through the middle of each ball. Balance the sticks across the top of a mug or glass, so that the beads are fully exposed to the air, and leave them to dry. They will be ready in about 24 hours.

4

Using a darning needle, thread the beads onto thin elastic until you have enough to go around your wrist comfortably. Knot the two ends of elastic together and trim the ends.

Ariel's tip:
The ocean shimmers with all the colours of the rainbow, so you can make these beads in any colour you like!

Aurora Royal Crown

Aurora wears her royal crown with pride. This crown is fit for a royal princess! You can be the ruler of your own princess kingdom!

You will need

- 8 x 11 inch tracing paper and pencil
- Strip of gold cardboard 5 x 24 inches
- Scissors, white glue and brush
- Hologram film 1 x 24 inches
- 2 strips of gold cardboard: 1½ x 13 inches
- Paperclips and paper fastener
- Purple felt
- Dinner plate
- Cotton batting
- Black acrylic paint and fine brush
- Assorted coloured gems

1

Trace the the crown template. Transfer it onto the back of the gold cardboard, then repeat, putting the second section up to the first. Cut out the whole strip.

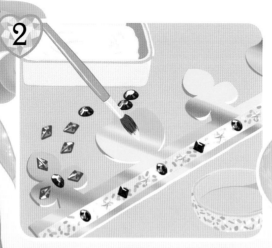

2

Glue the hologram film along the base, then glue gems along the top. Glue the two ends so the crown fits loosely on your head. Hold in place with paperclips. Let dry.

3

Push a paper fastener through where the strips meet.

Mark halfway between the shapes with the pencil. Glue the gold strips to the inside of the band where these marks are. Hold in place with paperclips. Let dry.

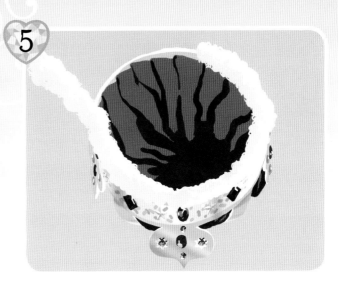

Trace around the dinner plate and cut out a circle of purple felt. Make small snips all around the outside of the felt circle. Glue the felt to the inner brim, gluing bit by bit along the clipped edge. Let dry.

Cut a strip of cotton batting about 2 inches (5cm) wide. Glue it along the bottom edge of the crown. Paint black spots about 1 inch (2.5cm) apart along the length of the cotton batting.

Aurora's tip:
Crown's are not only gold, but silver or pink, or any pretty colour you like!

Snow White

Friendship Bands

We all know Snow White has seven best friends! Show your best friend how much you like them with this great friendship band in pretty princess colours.

You will need

- 4 strands of cotton thread: 2 mauve, 1 pink and 1 purple (or the colours of your choice), each 20 inches (50 cm) long
- 1 large bead
- 4 medium-sized beads

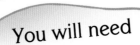

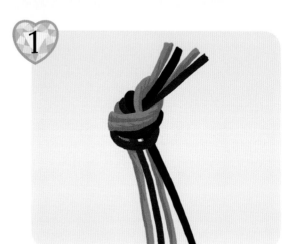

Take the 4 strands of cotton thread and knot them together, 8 inches (20cm) from one end.

Thread the large bead on the bracelet and push it up as far as the knot.

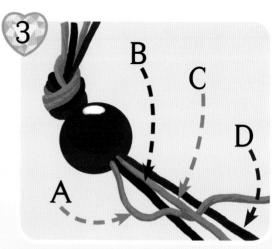

Spread out the 4 strands so that the 2 mauve strands are first and third from the left. Put A over B, under C and over D. Pull A gently to tighten the weave.

Continue weaving B over C, under D and over A, working over, under, over, under. Pull gently to tighten before starting on the next left-hand strand.

Continue weaving until you are about 3 inches (8cm) from the end, then tie the knotted strands into a knot, leaving the ends loose.

6

Thread a medium-sized bead onto each of the 4 loose strands and tie a knot to keep it in place.

Snow White's tip:
Give this band as a birthday present! Who would you give your band to?

Flower Garland

Make this beautiful flower necklace.
Be inspired by the colours in nature.

You will need

- 80 sheets of tissue paper in 2 different colours (40 of each) cut into squares of 8 x 8 inches (20 x 20cm)
- Bag of pipe cleaners
- Length of elastic or ribbon
- Scissors

1

Stack 4 sheets of one colour tissue paper together and fold over 5 times to make an accordian shape.

2

Cut both ends into a round shape then twist a pipe cleaner around the middle. Don't trim the ends of the pipe cleaner.

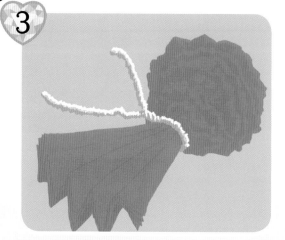

3

Gently separate out the tissue paper on both sides of the pipe cleaner into a flower shape.

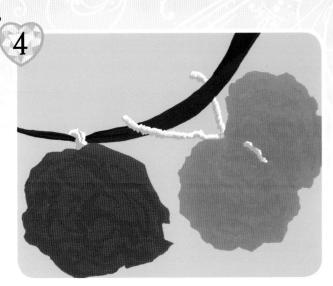

Twist the ends of the pipe cleaner around the ribbon or elastic and make sure the ends are not sticking out. Keep adding flowers until your garland is done.

Snow White's tip:
What's your favourite flower? Use this as inspiration for your garland!

Cinderella *Glitter Slippers*

With help from the fairy godmother Cinderella sparkled at the royal ball in her slippers. Now you can too, with these pretty glitter slippers!

Kids 1

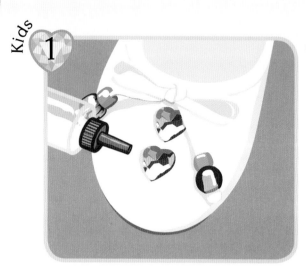

Glue the gems to the slipper and leave to dry.

Kids 2

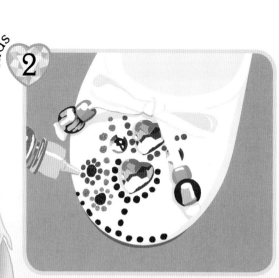

Next, add some more detail using the glitter glue. Gently make glittery dots on your shoes around the gems. Do one colour at a time and leave to dry before applying more.

You will need

- Pair of clean sneakers or canvas shoes
- Fabric paints
- Fabric pens
- Glitter
- Plastic gemstones
- Beads

Cinderella's tip:
You don't just have to try dots, you could draw flowers or hearts, or even write your name on your shoes!